CW01368377

Epstein-Barr Virus- A Holistic Approach to Healing

How to Mitigate its Impact & Reclaim Your Health

Candice Andrus, ND

DEDICATION

For my mother, Denise, my grandmother, Devota, my great-grandmother Lena, and all who've suffered and continue to suffer with chronic illness.

CONTENTS

PREFACE

I intend to show that expression of the Epstein-Barr virus depends on the condition of the body's inner terrain, which can be affected by nutritional status, environmental factors, and stress. I will discuss how the virus can affect our health, as well as how to minimize its impact through dietary, environmental, and lifestyle modifications in order to maintain or regain health. I will show that having EBV does not have to lead to further disease, and that we have more power over our health than what we've been led to believe.

1 INTRODUCTION

"Epstein-Barr Virus is an invasive and persistent virus- possibly one of the most common and detrimental viruses of our times with extremely high incidence of positive antibodies in all populations studied." Kasia Kines, Doctor of Clinical Nutrition

With chronic idiopathic illness (illness of an unknown origin or cause) at an all time high despite modern medicine's technological advances, it's probable that Epstein-Barr Virus (EBV) is an underlying factor in many of today's chronic illnesses. Yet it's not well understood and often overlooked by conventional medicine. In fact, many medical professionals only think of Epstein-Barr Virus as the cause of mononucleosis and aren't even aware that this virus can cause chronic symptoms long after someone recovers from mono. Mainstream medicine believes Chronic Active Epstein-Barr Virus (CAEBV) is rare and has little to offer those with chronic symptoms, but many integrative and functional medicine doctors as well as naturopaths and holistic practitioners believe it is more prevalent than most people realize. Unfortunately, too many people with chronic symptoms spend time and money searching for answers that the medical profession doesn't have. Patients are often dismissed by their doctor when test after test shows nothing is wrong. Others are given a diagnosis of a disease and then prescribed medications that not only don't address the root cause of their symptoms, but also lead to further problems. I am all too familiar with this scenario, as I, along with many of my clients and family members have been down this road.

Learning that I have EBV was a game changer for me. It suddenly became clear why my childhood was riddled with sickness, starting with severe colic as a baby, being hospitalized with pneumonia at 2, endless sinus and ear infections, strep throat and courses of antibiotics, chronic headaches, stomach problems, gastritis, and pain and numbness in my hands and arms. By the end of high school, I ended up with one of the most severe cases of mono my doctor had ever seen.

My twenties were full of frequent sinus infections that were treated with antibiotics several times a year. At 25, I was diagnosed with mono for the second time, which I thought wasn't possible. Recovering took months and I was left with chronic neck pain and fatigue. I went through the gamut of specialists and tests and was told there was nothing wrong. I was eventually diagnosed with fibromyalgia and prescribed an assortment of drugs, which only made me feel worse. I started reading everything I could about this "disease" and realized that the diagnosis was just a convenient way for my doctor to label a group of symptoms for which modern medicine didn't have an answer.

Fortunately my quest for answers led me to a chiropractor that motivated me to make better lifestyle choices. Once I started getting regular adjustments, the pain gradually began to lessen and I found the motivation to start exercising. I started making small changes in my diet and began to incorporate real food. Working out made me feel empowered, but often left me in extreme pain and seemed to weaken my system to the point where I'd frequently get sick and have to stop exercising. I didn't know at the time that intense exercise could lead to reactivation of the virus. I repeated the cycle on and off for years, but stayed motivated. As I learned more, I began to detoxify my body and found myself feeling better than I ever felt. I had officially reached "health nut" status.

Then my world came crashing down. I lost my mom from complications of a horrible autoimmune disease called Scleroderma and went through a difficult divorce. The grief and stress weakened my system and I ended up in a walk-in clinic with a sore throat, chronic fever, and swollen glands. The doctor suspected mono and I thought, " Not a third time!" Tests came back negative, but I felt like I had been run over by a truck. Fortunately, my cleaner diet and yoga routine made recovery quicker than it had been in the past.

It wasn't until ten years later that I was up against another battle with my health. I did everything I knew to do but wasn't getting better. I eventually discovered that the home my new husband and I lived in had significant levels of toxic mold. I learned that mold (especially the airborne mycotoxins it produces) is a big trigger for EBV reactivation. I was also under emotional stress at the time, so it was the perfect storm for the virus to reactivate. This time, addressing environmental factors and emotional health was just as necessary as diet and exercise for recovering my health.

My healing journey has been brutal at times, but has taught me to develop greater body awareness and to take control over my health through the choices I make. My nutrient deficient junk food diet and late nights eventually culminated in a severe case of mono. With each subsequent reactivation of EBV, I added another layer to my understanding about not only EBV, but also about immune health and viruses in general. Learning the truth about viruses was another game changer for me. Knowing that viruses exist within all of us and actually serve a beneficial purpose is highly empowering.

While diet, exercise, and adequate sleep are extremely important, they are not the whole picture. Addressing environmental factors and physical and emotional stress is equally important for good health. When it comes to chronic illness, I believe that Epstein-Barr Virus can be kept in check through nutritional, environmental, and lifestyle modifications, and that we all have the power to reclaim our health when we give the body what it needs and stop interfering with its attempts to heal. Health isn't a matter of luck, but a result of the choices we make on a daily basis about what we eat, how much and how we move, and even how we think. The silver lining in what I've gone through is that my experience with chronic illness allows me to have greater empathy and compassion for my clients be able to better support them on their healing journeys. If I was able to transform a like of sickness, pain, fatigue and depression to one of wellness, abundant energy, and joy, you can too.

What is Epstein-Barr Virus?

Epstein-Barr Virus (EBV), also known as human herpes virus 4, is a DNA lymphotropic herpes virus most known for being the causative agent of infectious mononucleosis, or mono. (Smatti, 2018) Lymphotropic viruses are those that have an affinity for lymphocytes (types of white blood cells). (Merriam-Webster.com, 2020) According to the CDC, Epstein-Barr Virus is one of the most common human viruses in the world, affecting at least 95% of the population. (CDC, 2016) However, most people don't even know they've been infected with the virus because they either have no symptoms or only mild symptoms that could be mistaken as a cold or flu. (Balch, 2010)

EBV is different from most infections that are conquered by our immune system. Instead, it hijacks our cells and uses them to replicate. By doing so, it protects itself from the immune system. After entering the body, the virus multiplies in B lymphocytes (white blood cells). The genetic material of EBV, known as an episome, is created in the B cells and stays in a dormant state in the cells for the rest of a person's life. (Glaser et. al., 1991 as cited in Kines, 2018) By hiding in the B cells, EBV is able to proliferate indefinitely, which is crucial for the pathogenesis of this virus. (Kerr, 2019)

How does someone get Epstein-Barr Virus?

It is thought that Epstein-Barr Virus is most commonly transmitted through saliva that contains infected epithelial cells, which is why mononucleosis was nicknamed the "Kissing Disease." (Smatti, 2018). Since healthy asymptomatic people can still shed the virus intermittently for years after the initial infection, it's easy to get EBV through kissing. (Kines, 2018) It can also be transmitted through blood transfusions and organ transplantations, and since infected epithelial cells can also be found in the uterine cervix and semen, it's possible that EBV can be spread through sexual contact. (Smatti, 2018) Anecdotal evidence shows that mothers can pass EBV to a fetus during pregnancy as well, so it's possible many of us are are born with the virus. Many people become infected with EBV as young children or as teenagers. As with other herpes viruses, a person can have an infection once and never have an episode again or the virus can reactivate and someone can have recurrent infections. (Kines, 2018)

Acute vs. Chronic Infection

Infection with EBV can have two outcomes. The first is a lytic (acute) infection in which EBV lyses (literally bursts out of) the host cells. (Eligio, 2010) The initial infection is often asymptomatic in children, but tends to develop into mono in 30-50% of adolescents. (De Paschale & Clerici, 2012) It is thought that adolescents may be more likely to be immune compromised due to a poor diet typical with teens, hormonal changes of puberty, and stress. (Kines, 2018) Mono typically presents with symptoms such as fever, sore throat, headache, body aches, puffy eyes, swollen glands, enlarged and/or painful spleen, and extreme fatigue, with symptoms lasting 2-4 weeks on average. (Balch, 2010).

After the initial infection, EBV is normally controlled by the immune system and the virus becomes dormant. As long as a person remains relatively healthy, the virus stays in this dormant state. If the immune system becomes weakened due to nutritional deficiencies, toxic exposure, hormone imbalances, other infections, immunosuppressive drugs, or stress, this can cause the virus to come out of hiding and begin to cause symptoms. Unfortunately, some people will experience extreme fatigue for several months to a year after the initial infection. Chronic mononucleosis syndrome is known to occur long term, with symptoms ranging from weakness, aching legs, low-grade fever (sometimes intermittent), depression, (Isaacs, 1984 as cited in Kines, 2018) as well as headaches, muscle pain, persistent fatigue, lymphadenopathy (a disease affecting lymph nodes), and a prolonged recovery period lasting more than the typical recovery period of about a month. (Eligio, 2010)

The second outcome is Chronic Active Epstein-Barr Virus (CAEBV)- a latent chronic infection. (Kines, 2018) According to the National Institutes of Health, CAEBV occurs when the EBV infection doesn't go away and the virus remains active, with symptoms persisting and becoming worse over time. (NIH) This isn't necessarily the case, though, as many people experience only periodic reactivation throughout their lives. Since the virus is pleomorphic (of different forms), it can switch from dormant to active at any time, infecting the B cells (and/or T cells) and hiding inside them, thus eluding the immune system and replicating inside the cells until the time comes to lyse again and re-infect the person. This process is not spontaneous, but is driven by external factors. (Kines, 2018)

The most common symptoms of CAEBV are: fever, swollen lymph nodes, enlarged liver, enlarged spleen, anemia, nerve damage, liver failure, and pneumonia. (NIH) However, newer, varied and seemingly unrelated symptoms can arise, as the virus moves into different organs. Hypersensitivity to mosquito bites has even been reported to be characteristic of CAEBV. (Kawamoto et. al., 2018) Many people who suffer with chronic unexplained symptoms don't even realize they are experiencing a reactivation of EBV. According to research, "Chronic activated EBV can be expected in chronic illness, which cannot be explained by other disease processes at diagnosis." (Eligio, 2010)

Implications for Long-term Health

Despite the fact that most health care practitioners are not aware of the dangers of CAEBV, there is considerable evidence linking the virus to chronic illness and serious diseases. In a study of 30 people with CAEBV over a 68-month period, 10 people died of liver failure, malignant lymphoma, or other causes, which is a 33.3% death rate. (Kimura, 2001 as cited in Kines, 2018) The body uses CD8+T cells, types of white blood cells, to keep the virus in check. If there is an impairment or deficiency of these cells, the virus can reactivate. (Carnahan) CD8+T cell deficiency has been linked to age, estrogen levels, vitamin D deficiency, certain medications, and poor immune function, and is thought to underlie the development of chronic autoimmune diseases by impairing CD8+T cell control of EBV. (Pender, 2012) CAEBV reactivation is an important mechanism in the pathogenesis of many diseases. Not only that, but even latent EBV infection has been linked to disease states. In the case of EBV, latent does not mean inactivated since EBV replicates inside the infected B cells mainly by the latent mechanism. However, these infected B cells will only lyse and infect other cells in the lytic phase (acute reinfection). (Kines, 2018)

Reactivation has been shown to occur in people with a variety of cancers, autoimmune diseases, chronic fatigue syndrome, myalgic encephalitis, and other circumstances such as being an inpatient in an ICU. (Kerr, 2019) Any other infection can also induce EBV reactivation, whether it's bacterial, viral or fungal. (Kines, 2018) Inflammation and chemical agents or drugs, especially immunosuppressive drugs can also lead to a reactivation. (Smatti, 2018) Not only does CAEBV occur more often in immune-compromised people, but it has also been causally related to many diseases. Here are some of the more common illnesses found to be connected with EBV:

Chronic Fatigue Syndrome

Studies show that a small percentage of patients with infectious mononucleosis will not recover and will develop Chronic Fatigue Syndrome (CFS), which may be what has sometimes been referred to as chronic mononucleosis. It is established that CFS commonly follows an acute viral infection. (Lancet, 2010 as cited in Kines, 2018) CFS, characterized by extreme fatigue that can't be explained by an underlying medical condition, used to be called "chronic Epstein-Barr syndrome." (Buchwald, 1987 as cited in Kines, 2018)

Autoimmune Disorders

Chronic infections may play a role in autoimmune conditions by keeping the body in a state of low-level alarm, which activates the body's stress response and leads to dysregulation of the immune system. (Romm) "Viral infection, including Epstein-Barr Virus, is one of the most frequently considered environmental factors involved in autoimmunity." (Janegova et al., 2015) Multiple Sclerosis has been linked to EBV in multiple studies. "Epstein-Barr Infection as indicated by positive serology is an obligatory precondition for multiple sclerosis, which is a stronger attribute than a risk factor only." (Jons, 2015 as cited in Kines, 2018) There is an established epidemiological link between herpes virus infection and risk of MS. (Tarlinton, 2020) In fact, those with a history of infectious mononucleosis have a two-three-fold increase in lifetime risk of multiple sclerosis. (Crawford, 2014) Among some of the other autoimmune disorders linked to EBV are: Atherosclerosis, Celiac, Diabetes Type 1, Guillian-Barre Syndrome, Hashimoto's Thyroiditis, Chrohn's and Ulcerative Colitis, Psoriasis, Rheumatoid Arthritis, Scleroderma, Sjogren's, and Systemic Lupus. (Kines, 2018)

Cancer

Since it's discovery in 1964, EBV's status as the first human tumor virus has been firmly established. The first cancer found to be linked to EBV was Burkitt's Lymphoma. (Crawford, et. al., 2014) Since then, it's been well documented that Nasopharyngeal Carcinoma, Hodgkin and Non-Hodgkin Lymphoma, Stomach Cancer, and many other forms of cancer have been either caused by or associated with EBV. (Kines, 2018) It is estimated that over 200,000 new cases of cancer a year are linked to tumors caused by EBV. (Shannon-Lowe & Rickinson, 2019) EBV-carriers are 15 times more likely to develop some form of cancer than those who don't have the virus. Still, rare circumstances can allow that oncogenic potential to be realized and only a small fraction of the virus-carrying population ever develops a virus-associated tumor. (Crawford et. al., 2014)

Of course we can't forget about the many people who haven't been given a label for their chronic symptoms, yet continue to suffer without knowing they have EBV. When we consider all the diseases that EBV is linked to, especially the fact that it's known to be oncogenic, it paints a dismal picture for those with the virus. However, this is not meant to scare the reader, but to bring awareness of the potential this virus has when we provide it with an environment favorable for disease development. Fortunately, as you will read, there are proven ways to decrease the potential dangers of this virus.

How does someone know they have Epstein-Barr Virus?

If someone has ever had mononucleosis, they have antibodies to the virus. Diagnosing mono is simple enough. A blood test called a mononucleosis spot test is all that's needed. (Balch, 2010) Confirming that someone has CAEBV, on the other hand, can be a bit tricky since it can be difficult to determine if the virus has become reactivated. According to the National Institutes of Health, CAEBV is diagnosed using a quantitative PCR test showing high EBV DNA in the blood for at least 3 months. (NIH) However, Dr. Kasia Kines, Doctor of Clinical Nutrition and author of *The Epstein-Barr Virus Solution*, points out that because there is a rapid decline in viral load within 2-25 days of infection as the virus moves to organs, PCR tests are not very effective for diagnosing chronic and reactivated EBV. (Kines, 2018) Serological diagnosis is commonly used to determine EBV infection, with VCA-IgG antibodies detection being the best single serological test to indicate a past exposure. (Smatti, 2018) However, since not all people with a current EBV infection show positive antibodies, testing isn't always accurate. This is why Dr. Kines recommends VCA-IgM, EA-D IgG, and EBNA IgG testing as well. (Kines, 2018) In addition, many doctors will dismiss the significance of finding positive antibodies because they consider it a past infection that couldn't possibly be causing current symptoms. However, it's important to know that lab tests that suggest past infection may actually indicate a long-term latent infection, which is "the preferred driver of EBV sustainability in our body." (Kines, 2018, p. 36)

Although more researchers are becoming aware that stubborn medical cases are possibly linked to hidden CAEBV, there is still a lot of confusion and uncertainty in both the mainstream and alternative medical communities about the testing and treatment of CAEBV. There are no standardized tests, and many doctors are unwilling to test for EBV antibodies, so it can be a frustrating experience for someone to confirm they have the virus. Fortunately, people now have access to online labs directly. For those who've been unable to find answers to chronic health problems, it can be a relief to learn what's been the cause of their suffering. Knowing what's at the root of a diagnosis or unexplained symptoms can empower people to take the steps needed to regain their health.

Allopathic Medicine's Approach to Epstein-Barr Virus

Conventional medicine's approach to dealing with EBV is to treat symptoms. For acute symptoms, doctors typically recommend over the counter pain relievers, and some may prescribe antibiotics, since bacterial infections often go hand in hand with viral infections. Practitioners who do recognize CAEBV often prescribe medications to manage symptoms even though research has shown that antiviral therapy is usually ineffective. Although anecdotal reports have shown acyclovir may have some antiviral activity in some cases, researchers have found a lack of response to antiviral therapy in most cases. Likewise, anecdotal reports suggest that CAEBV may respond to immune-modulatory agents, but these have also been found to be ineffective. Not only that, but they can inhibit immune response to EVB and may allow virus-infected cells to proliferate further. While patients may have a temporary response to treatments such as Rituximab, immunosuppressive therapy, cytotoxic chemotherapy, autologous CTLs, or syngeneic HSCT, these treatments are not curative. (Cohen, 2011) The only proven effective treatment is hematopoietic stem cell transplantations. (Kimura, 2017) Another extreme therapy, bone marrow transplant, has been documented in two life-threatening cases. (Miyamura, 2008) Current research is focused on immune defects and genetic abnormalities linked to CAEBV. (Cohen, 2009)

Because EBV is linked to such an astounding number of diseases, the goal of the EBV research community is to lessen the disease burden by preventing the infection altogether with a vaccine. The question is, will the risks of a vaccine be worth the benefits, especially when there is already evidence that vaccines have caused even further harm to immune compromised people and those with existing health problems? In 2007, GlaxoSmithKline tried to develop a recombinant vaccine. In a randomized, double blind, placebo controlled trial, eight of the placebo group developed infectious mononucleosis compared to just two of the vaccine group. By the end of the 18-month trial, 9 of the placebo and 11 of the vaccinated group showed silent primary EBV infection. While vaccination appeared to reduce symptoms, it did not prevent the infection itself. (Sokal et. al., 2007 as cited in Crawford et. al., 2014)

It is the medical community's position that there is nothing that can be done for CAEBV other than managing symptoms and that a vaccine is the only hope. This view is disempowering for patients and provides no solutions. With 95% of the population carrying the virus and many with no symptoms, a vaccine doesn't seem like a logical answer. I will provide a more empowered way of looking at the virus by showing that there are scientifically validated natural therapies to help prevent it from becoming harmful.

Holistic Approach to Epstein-Barr Virus

In contrast to conventional medicine's view of EBV, practitioners in the functional, integrative, and naturopathic medical field seek to address the underlying cause of dysfunction rather than just treat symptoms. Functional and integrative medicine may use a combination of drug based and natural therapies, but the naturopathic approach is to support the body with nutritional therapies and educate people about self-healing and self-care. This approach seeks to balance the body's internal environment so it isn't favorable for the virus to reproduce and cause harm. Naturopathy approaches healing from a holistic perspective with the understanding that the body, mind, and soul are connected, and that reclaiming health involves healing the gut and supporting the immune system, optimizing detoxification pathways and reducing the body's toxic load, and addressing stress and other lifestyle factors.

While conventional medicine is focused on the possibility of genetic abnormalities associated with CAEBV, naturopathy focuses on a more empowered way of managing the virus by helping people understand why they are sick and how to regain health by using methods that support the body's own healing capacity. Researchers may find more genetic predispositions, but thanks to the field of epigenetics, we now know that something in our environment must activate these genes. Even if there is a genetic component involved in the susceptibility of developing CAEBV, it doesn't necessarily mean that specific genes will automatically lead to CAEBV. Our environment, the toxins we are exposed to, the nutrients we absorb, our hormones, and the chemical messages our bodies receive based on the way we think or feel can all determine whether a gene will be expressed or not. Instead of thinking of ourselves as being at the mercy of our genetics, we need to be aware of how our choices affect our biology. (Lipton, 2015)

2 IMPORTANCE OF IMMUNE FUNCTION

If I could live my life over again, I would devote it to proving that germs seek their natural habitat- diseased tissue; e.g., mosquitoes seek the stagnant water but do not cause the pool to be stagnant." Rudolph Virchow (Father of Pathology)

If Epstein-Barr virus is so dangerous, how is it that almost the entire population has the virus, yet not everyone experiences symptoms or develops a life-threatening disease? To understand why, it's important to know how the body's immune system responds to this virus that tricks its way into the very cells that are supposed to control it. Here is the paradox of EBV: Although the body has a massive immune response when first infected, the body never clears the virus. When someone gets infected, whether they develop mono or not, some EBV-infected B lymphocytes always survive, and the person carries the virus for life. "A fine balance has been struck between virus and host, one that allows this potentially dangerous infection to persist without threatening the life of its host." (Crawford et al., 2014, p. 108) This coexistence between virus and host depends on the host's immune system being able to keep it from reactivating. A strong immune system may not protect us from EBV, but it does protect us from developing CAEBV. The virus hides in the B lymphocytes waiting for the right opportunity to become active again. Once the virus reemerges from it's hiding place, EBV-specific T lymphocytes go to work to prevent the reemerging virus from becoming too dangerous. (Crawford et. al., 2014)

If the immune system is weakened, the virus is able to rapidly proliferate and has the potential to become dangerous, leading to chronic degenerative disorders. Recent research suggests that the condition of the body's inner terrain is what is behind most symptoms. (Young, 2001) Conventional medicine is narrowly focused on killing microbes and managing symptoms, while ignoring the terrain. Naturopathy, on the other hand, focuses on the bigger picture- that is, how the expression of the virus depends on the condition of the terrain. The scientific community may focus on either rare genetic mutations or drugs that impair the immune response as the primary drivers of EBV related cancers, (Crawford et. al., 2014) but naturopathy has a different view of immune function.

Germ Theory

Germ theory was developed by French chemist Louis Pasteur and German physician Robert Koch. It claims disease is primarily caused by bacteria and viruses. (Lipton, 2015) After injecting healthy animals with the blood of sick animals, causing the injected animals to get sick, Pasteur postulated that germs caused disease. The concept of specific, unchanging types of germs as the cause of disease, also known as monomorphism (one-formism), was accepted by the emerging field of allopathic medicine in the late 19th century. Monomorphism, the idea that "all microorganisms are fixed species, unchangeable; that each pathological type produces only one specific disease; that microorganisms never arise endogenously (originate inside the host); and that blood and tissues are sterile under healthy conditions" became the basis for the new field of virology. (Young, 2001, p. 247) While theoretically the blood may be sterile in ideal health conditions, it has the potential to develop morbid microorganisms.

Terrain Theory

Pasteur's counterparts believed that the inner condition of the body was more important than the germ. Thirty years before the germ theory was accepted by mainstream medicine, Antoine Bechamp formulated the mycrozymian principle, also known as pleomorphism (pleo = many; morph = form) as the basis for terrain theory. Mycrozymas are tiny indestructible living elements found in all living things, including human cells, that are capable of producing enzymes, fermenting sugar, and evolving into more complex forms. Bechamp's assertion was that microzymas exist within living organisms both to build cells and eventually the whole organism and to recycle the physical body when it dies. Bechamp viewed the life process as a "continual cellular breakdown by microzymian fermentation-even in a healthy body," and theorized that disease is a "condition of one's internal environment (terrain); that disease (and it's symptoms) are born of us and in us; and that disease is not produced by an attack of microentities but calls forth their endogenous evolution." (Young, 2001, p. 248) In a healthy individual, mycrozymas act harmoniously. In a diseased state, they evolve into morbidly evolved microzymas, or germs. The cause of morbid evolution, he claimed, is "modification of our terrain by an inverted way of eating and living." (Young, 2011, p. 27)

Another of Pasteur's contemporaries was Claude Bernard, a French physiologist who saw disease as an underlying condition, rather than the symptoms that are diagnosed or the germs involved. (Becker, 1985 as cited in Young, 2001) Bernard popularized the term "terrain" to describe the internal environment of the body. "A healthy or diseased terrain is determined primarily be four things: it's acid/alkaline balance (pH), its electric/magnetic charge (negative or positive), it's level of poisoning (toxicity), and its nutritional status." (Young, 2001, p. 21) Germs thrive in an unbalanced terrain and stimulate the development of symptoms. According to Bernard, low oxygen, stagnation of colloidal body fluids, and loss of electrical charge on the surface of red blood cells are symptoms of a diseased terrain. Bernard was so confident that germs do not cause disease that he reportedly told a group of doctors and scientists, "The terrain is everything, the germ is nothing," as he drank a glass of water with cholera bacteria in it without getting sick. (Young, 2011, p. 67)

While learning to clone cells in graduate school, biologist Bruce Lipton, PhD, confirmed that the terrain was indeed the determining factor in the health of cells. He learned that when cultured cells being studied are ailing, to look first to the cell's environment, not the cell itself, for the cause. When he provided a healthy environment for cells, they thrived, but when the environment wasn't optimal, they faltered. When he adjusted the environment, the ailing cells revitalized. (Lipton, 2015)

Through the use of live blood cell analysis, Dr. Robert Young, Ph.D., D.Sc., author of *Sick and Tired*, confirmed the existence of microzymas in the blood and found that they can either evolve or devolve depending on the conditions of the terrain. Live-cell analysis is able to clearly show bacterial, yeast, fungal forms, and mold coming out of red and white blood cells that initially appeared normal. As conditions of the terrain deteriorate, red and white blood cells evolve into morbid forms. The developmental cycle that takes place in a sick body begins with repair proteins evolving into bacteria, then into yeast and fungal forms, and eventually into mold. Dr. Young observed the evolution of pleomorphic organisms in people with seemingly unrelated and separate medical diagnoses. In each case, he saw the same microorganisms in those with EBV, Diabetes, Breast Cancer, and AIDS and witnessed these organisms evolve into fungal balls. (Young, 2001)

Dr. Young's research demonstrates that the complexes science refers to as viruses actually originate in the cell, as microzymian principle suggests. Viruses appear to be repair proteins that evolved from microzymas created in response to a diseased condition for the purpose of genetic repair and destruction of diseased tissue, not pathogenic organisms that merely cause symptoms. Something in the cell produces or becomes a virus for a beneficial purpose and once the virus is there, it can evolve into a morbid form if the conditions of the terrain are not healthy. In an unbalanced terrain, the breakdown of bodily tissue by the putrefaction of bacteria and fermentation of yeast and fungus is accelerated. (Young, 2001) Symptoms are not a direct result of the virus at work, but the result of the immune system's production of inflammatory cytokines (Nathan, 2018) and the decomposition of bodily tissues. (Young, 2001) It's the breakdown of bodily tissue that creates acid waste products and causes symptoms. In other words, the body is decomposing while still living. (Young, 2001)

Germ Theory Vs. Terrain Theory

The pleomorphic theory challenges the monomorphic theory that says all disease starts with germs from outside the body. While there are outside forces that do affect health, a large number of disease states result from within. The science of pleomorphism has demonstrated that every cell has a healthy and an unhealthy form. Bernard pointed out that Pasteur's animal experiment was not a scientific procedure and it only showed that an individual can be made sick by poisoning the blood. Poisoning the animal's terrain led to diseased tissues, which allowed germs to proliferate. Pasteur was confusing disease with its symptoms. Not only that, but the method of injection does not duplicate a natural infection. Pasteur himself was reported to have admitted on his deathbed, "Claude Bernard was right- the microbe is nothing, the terrain is everything." (Young, 2001, p. 28) Even though the germ theory was not based in solid science, this monomorphic view unfortunately took hold and set the stage for cancer and degenerative diseases due to a lack of true understanding of infectious diseases. It remains the basis for modern medicine today and is a major block to resolving chronic illness.

Role of pH in Immune Function

Metabolic processes depend on the chemical balance between acid and alkaline conditions in the blood and tissues. This delicate balance greatly affects the condition of the terrain, and the body continuously tries to maintain homeostasis. The body's pH is influenced by our diet, lifestyle, environment and even our thoughts. When the body's fluid and tissue pH shifts to an acid state, it creates a favorable environment for healthy cells to evolve into unhealthy cells. The acidic by-products produced by these morbidly evolved cells add to the acidification of the body. A chronic acidic condition and oxygen deprivation in the blood and tissues caused by too much acid-forming food, poor lifestyle, as well as environmental and emotional stress increases susceptibility to viral infections because it requires the body to work harder to maintain homeostasis. (Young, 2001). Low pH actually makes it easier for EBV to fuse with the host cell. According to one study, the fusion "at pH 5.9 was significantly enhanced compared to that at neutral pH." (Pozzi et. al., 1992)

Acidification of the terrain initiates the process of bodily decomposition, leading to disease by corroding the tissues and eventually interrupting all cellular functions. "Acidification/hypoxia biochemically signals a dead host to the microzyma, while creating collapsed areas (dead zones)" and "is the primary physiological disease condition out of which the symptoms commonly caused diseases arise." (Young, 2001, p. 250) A change in terrain caused by toxic overload of the cell happens prior to the appearance of viruses. It is likely that cancerous development is cell conversion from primarily oxidative to fermentative metabolism, mediated by fungus and mold. (Young, 2001) Thus, the development of cancer appears to be more directly linked to terrain condition than to EBV itself.

In allopathic medicine, disease begins at the onset of symptoms. However, with the theories of Béchamp followed by the verifiable scientific research of Professor Gunter Enderlein, who tested and proved Béchamp's theories, we have a more accurate definition of disease. Disease begins when our alkaline tissues turn acidic causing inflammation, our negative energy charge turns positive, and when our biome becomes imbalanced. (Young, 2001) In his Textbook of Medical Physiology (once used in medical schools), Dr. Arthur Guyton stated, "The first step to maintaining health is to alkalize the body. The second step is to increase the number of negative hydrogen ions. These are the two most important aspects of homeostasis." (Batt, 2016)

Terrain Theory and Immunity

Fighting germs is not the immune system's primary job. Its main job is to act as an inner janitor, recycling and discarding the body's own metabolic waste and cellular debris. The immune system is only a backup system that takes over when the terrain is compromised and fails to keep harmful organisms from proliferating. When the gut mucosal barrier is not compromised, the immune system doesn't have to step in to deal with germs and is better able to do its primary job. Thus, a balanced terrain is the primary defense against disease. Dr. Young refers to the over reliance on the immune system to ward off pathogens as "riding around on a spare tire" all the time, and says the misplaced emphasis on stimulating immune function is an "unfortunate hangover from germ theory." (Young, 2001, p. 33) Still, because most people today and especially those with CAEBV have compromised gut linings, supporting immune function using natural interventions is often necessary for healing. The ultimate goal, though, should be to balance the terrain so the immune system can do a better job of handling the body's waste, which will in turn keep pathogens in check.

If we consider EBV in terms of terrain theory, we can take a more empowered stance by recognizing the effects our own choices have over how the virus behaves. When we realize viruses are the first stage of cellular evolution, we can view EBV as a friend instead of foe, seeing symptoms as warnings of impending danger due to changes in the terrain. If mold, yeast, and fungi are precursors for cancer, then it's plausible that by preventing these morbid evolutions by maintaining a healthy terrain, EBV cannot act as an oncogenic agent. To link EBV with various cancers and other diseases without considering this crucial piece of the puzzle does a disservice to those seeking answers about how to heal. With an understanding of how the terrain affects immune function, it's possible to prevent disease processes. Let's look at 3 key factors that can affect the terrain and lead to viral reactivation, along with proven strategies to keep the virus in check.

3 ROLE OF NUTRITION

"One personal choice seems to influence long-term health prospects more than any other- what we eat." C. Everett Koop, M.D. Surgeon General

Nutritional status is a critical factor in whether or not EBV remains dormant. Adequate intake of micronutrients is required for proper immune function. According to Dr. Kines, the virus becomes more virulent in nutritionally compromised people. (Kines, 2018) Nutritional deficiencies can be triggered by oxidative stress, which in turn impairs immune function. (Vasquez 2014). By driving viral activity and causing damage and mutation of EBV's DNA, free radical damage and oxidative stress cause the virus to be more aggressive. Thus, "a normally avirulent virus becomes virulent because of changes in the viral genome." (Kines, 2018) The Standard American Diet (SAD) causes oxidative stress, systemic inflammation, and activation of Nuclear Factor kappa B (NFkB), a multi-protein complex that acts as an inflammatory agent and drives viral replication. This leads to changes in the terrain that support the development of viral infection. (Vasquez, 2014) Just one meal including an egg and sausage muffin sandwich and two hash browns has been shown to increase NFkB for two hours, causing increased oxidative stress. (Aljada et al., 2004 as cited in Vasquez, 2014)

EBV itself also creates high levels of oxidative stress in the body, which leads to the release of inflammatory cytokines. Inflammatory cytokines are signaling molecules secreted from immune cells that promote inflammation, play a role in initiating the inflammatory response and regulating the immune system's defense against pathogens. (Kines, 2018) Excessive amounts of inflammatory cytokines have been shown to worsen symptoms and lead to fever, inflammation, and tissue destruction.

(Dinarello, 2000)

Add to this, the fact that most people today are nutritionally deficient as a result of poor food choices and nutritionally depleted soil, and we have a recipe for chronic illness. Because of decades of unsustainable farming practices, our soil is not as rich in nutrients as it once was; thus, our food has also become less nutritious than it was even one generation ago. In addition, the food supply is laden with pesticide residues, hormones, and genetically modified organisms that interfere with important physiological functions. Research is clear that commercially grown produce has lower nutrient density, on top of being contaminated with pesticide residues. Reviews of multiple studies show that organic varieties provide significantly greater levels of vitamin C, iron, magnesium and phosphorus than non-organic varieties of the same foods. While being higher in these nutrients, they are also significantly lower in nitrates and pesticide residues. (Kines, 2018) In addition, with the exception of wheat, oats, and wine, organic foods typically provide greater levels of a number of important antioxidant phytochemicals (anthocyanins, flavonoids, and carotenoids). (Crinnion, 2010)

According to Dr. Aviva Romm, it's definitely possible to send EBV into dormancy and remain symptom free using natural methods. In fact, the virus is one of the most reversible causes of Hashimoto's she sees in her practice. (Romm, 2020) Because CAEBV hasn't been the focus of mainstream medicine or nutrition, there were no strategic nutritional guidelines on how to treat it until recently. Thanks to the work of Dr. Alex Vasquez, D.C., N.D., D.O., F.A.C.N., who did an intensive review of literature on viral physiology, pathology, and natural antiviral nutrients and botanicals, clinicians now have clearly defined nutritional strategies for helping people with viral infections. Dietary modifications will support immune function and the clearance of viral infection. By using antiviral nutrients, we can modify DNA expression and viral replication. We can also support metabolic functions to minimize the consequences of viral infections. (Vasquez, 2014) Based on the available literature, it appears that maintaining strong immune function, minimizing oxidative stress, free radical damage and inflammation, and supporting the body with antiviral nutrients are all key to keeping EBV at bay. (Kines, 2018)

Dietary Modifications

The nutritional protocol developed by Dr. Vasquez is validated by biochemistry, physiology, experimental research, peer-reviewed human trials, and the clinical application of common sense. His approach helps restore optimal physiological function by replenishing essential nutrients, balancing hormones, promoting detoxification of environmental toxins, eliminating gut dysbiosis, and restoring optimal microbial balance. Based on the literature, a Paleo-Mediterranean Diet, which combines the Paleolithic and Mediterranean diets (both of which have been well studied) is beneficial for most. It includes abundant amounts of fruits, vegetables, seeds, nuts, omega-3 and monounsaturated fatty acids, and lean sources of protein such as lean meats, fatty cold-water fish, and whey proteins. Overconsumption of chemical preservatives, artificial sweeteners, and processed high-glycemic carbohydrate foods are prohibited. According to Dr. Vasquez, this diet supports and empowers immune function due to the high intake of micronutrients, phytonutrients, and the alkalizing pro-homeostatic benefits in addition to the absence of nutrient-poor high carbohydrate and high fat foods which are immunosuppressive and pro-inflammatory. The Mediterranean diet has shown unparalleled safety and efficacy in prevention of heart disease, cancer, and all-cause mortality, but hasn't been studied specifically for addressing viral infection. Although not studied specifically for EBV, Dr. Vasquez points out that absence of direct evidence does not indicate a lack of antiviral benefits for those with EBV and that the inference of reduction of all-cause mortality by the Mediterranean diet implies a reduction in infection-related mortality. (Vasquez, 2014)

Dr. Kines agrees that a diet rich in fruits and vegetables will keep inflammation down and provide essential nutrients to keep the virus in a dormant state. Antioxidant rich fruits and vegetables should be the foundation of an antiviral approach to diet. She suggests focusing on fresh, organic fruits and veggies, some organic whole grains, nuts and seeds, legumes, and limited amounts of cold-water wild-caught fish, wild game or grass-fed meat and avoiding specific "diets" or eating trends. Light meals, vegetable broths and soups, steamed vegetables, short grain brown rice or congee, and some raw vegetables if tolerated are best for those who are trying to heal. With a chronic or inflammatory illness, it's helpful to eliminate inflammatory foods like corn, dairy, and gluten, as well as vegetable oils like canola, safflower, soy, and corn oil, as they do not promote healing or repair but can contribute to or trigger illness. It's important, though, to avoid going to extremes and cutting out entire food groups, as restrictive diets followed long term can lead to nutrient deficiencies. Close to 80% of chronic medical conditions stem from nutrient deficiencies. (Kines, 2018) Since nutrient deficiencies can cause the virus to become more virulent, it's best not to be overly restrictive.

Diet and pH

PH is an important consideration when it comes to diet because a balanced pH is necessary for nutrient assimilation. The process of digestion, or fermentation, breaks down the food we eat into usable nutrients. What's left is an ash residue that combines with our bodily fluids to form an acid or alkaline pH. Foods are either acid forming or alkaline forming. A primarily acidic diet such as the Standard American Diet (SAD) creates inflammation and stress on the body. In general, animal products, dairy, processed, fermented, and refined foods are acid forming. Grains, with the exception of buckwheat and spelt, are acid forming. Vegetable juices and many vegetables such as cucumber, onion, and garlic are very alkalizing. Low-sugar fruits such as lemon, lime, tomato, and avocado are also alkalizing. Dr. Young suggests a 4 to 1 alkaline/acid intake ratio as a general guideline. For those who have an overgrowth of yeast or fungus, he recommends a 3 to 1 ratio since these morbid forms produce acid and add to the acidic condition the body is already in. The goal is to get the body back into a slightly alkaline condition that doesn't support the development of morbid microorganisms. The quickest way to correct an overly acidic condition is with fresh green drinks, juices and foods. Maintaining a balanced pH places less stress on the body. (Young, 2001)

Dr. Jill Carnahan echoes this line of thinking. The goal is to suppress and try to eliminate the virus and boost immune function by creating an environment within the body where the virus cannot thrive.

She says the best way to tackle EBV is similar to how she deals with an imbalance of gut microbes in her practice. The most important thing is to balance the inner terrain to support natural immunity and decrease exposure to environmental toxins and other infections. By balancing the condition of the body, the virus can be kept in check. (Carnahan)

NFkB Modulation

Another important consideration is the role Nuclear Factor kappa B (NFkB) plays in promoting inflammation. Pharmaceutical companies are trying to develop synthetic inhibitors of NFkB that will likely succeed, but will come with plenty of adverse effects. Because NFkB also plays a role in a wide range of healthy bodily processes, including immune response to infectious diseases, there is a strong possibility that a drug will negatively impact health. It is wiser to instead try to modulate its function, rather than suppress its function altogether. This can be done with several natural interventions including vitamin D, curcumin (requires piperine for absorption), lipoic acid, green tea, rosemary, grape seed extract, propolis, zinc, high-dose selenium, indole-3-carbinol, N-acetyl-L-cysteine, and resveratrol. (Vasquez, 2014)

Methylation Support

DNA methylation support is another important factor in keeping the virus in check. EBV genes can be turned off by nutrient modulation. Viral DNA sequences must be turned on by transcription factors such as NFkB. DNA methylation involves tagging these sequences with a molecule with a methyl group, which turns off genes so that they are not expressed. (Vasquez, 2014) "It is well established that methylation plays a critical role in EBV gene silencing." (Hughes, 2012 as cited in Kines, 2018) Hypo-methylation increases not only EBV replication, but also increases the risk of autoimmune disorders and cancer, so it's important to address this issue. To optimize methylation, methyl-donating/transferring nutrients such as folate, betaine, vitamin B6, vitamin B12 (methylcobalamin), and NAC are necessary but not sufficient, according to Dr. Vasquez. Other nutrients including vitamin D3 also play an important role in promoting methylation. However, the process of methylation is heavily influenced by environmental factors like xenobiotic/toxin exposure, UV light exposure, and certain pharmaceutical drugs. Thus, a combination of nutritional interventions and avoidance of chemical, pollution and drug exposure is also critical. (Vasquez, 2014)

Antiviral Foods

While few foods have been studied specifically for anti-EBV activity, there are some listed here:

Sulforaphane (SFN)- This compound in cruciferous vegetables like Brussels sprouts, broccoli, cauliflower, cabbage, Bok Choy, kale, watercress, collards, and radishes shows antiviral qualities. In one study, SFN was found to be effective in inhibiting EBV reactivation. (Wu et al., 2013)

Resveratrol- This antioxidant found in red grapes inhibits the transcription of lytic genes and EBV's lytic cycle to reduce the production of viral particles. This suggests that resveratrol may be useful to prevent the proliferation of the virus. (Yui et al., 2010)

Citrus Fruit Peel and Seed Extract- Citrus peels and seeds also show antiviral activity against EBV. Extracts of fruit peels and seeds from 78 species of Citrus were found to inhibit EBV early antigen (EBV-EA) activation. (Iwase et. al., 1999)

Green Tea- Epigallocatechin gallate (EGCG) in green tea inhibits EBV reactivation, in addition to being a potent antimicrobial compound. At concentrations exceeding 50mcg, EGCG inhibits the expression of EBV lytic proteins and inhibits the initiation of the EBV lytic cascade. (Chang et. al., 2003)

Garlic- While no studies have been done on the use of garlic for EBV specifically, it has been used for centuries for its antibiotic, antifungal, and antiviral qualities. In one study, fresh garlic extract was shown to kill every virus it was exposed to. (Weber et. al., 1992)

Antiviral Nutrients

Selenium, vitamin C, vitamin E, vitamin A, caprylic acid, undecylenic acid, butyric acid, lauric acid, N-acetyl cysteine, L-taurine, germanium, cat's claw, pycnogenol and colloidal silver all have antiviral, antifungal and anti-mycotoxic properties and are important in restoring immune function by combatting fungus- producing mycotoxins, according to Dr. Young. (Young, 2001) Dr. Vasquez has found direct antiviral nutritional support, nutrients and herbs that prevent viral replication, nutritional support for immune modulation, methylation, and cell system support to be successful. (Vasquez, 2014) The following are research-supported supplements for EBV:

Vitamin A- Retinoic Acid has been shown to inhibit EBV induction. (Yamamoto et al., 1979 as cited in Kines, 2018)

Vitamin D- Vitamin D has direct anti-viral effects. (Beard et. al, 2011) Numerous studies show Vitamin D to be one of the most powerful means for enhancing immunity and avoiding diseases by reorganizing the pattern of methylation and gene expression. (Zhu et. al., 2013) High dose vitamin D3 has been shown to affect humoral immune response to the latent EBV antigen. (Rosjo, et al., 2017)

Vitamin E- Vitamin E is a potent antioxidant that was shown to reduce NFkB activity to decrease viral replication, rapidly reducing splenomegalies in EBV infected people. (Flavin et. al., 2006) Vitamin E was also shown to completely inhibit oncogene LMP1 in EBV infected B cells, proving that it is able to block EBV induced oxidative stress. (Chen et al., 2003)

Selenium- Selenium is well studied for its antiviral and immune-supportive properties. (Beck, 2001 as cited in Kines, 2018) One study showed that selenium inhibits EBV early antigens. (Jian et. al., 2003)

Lysine- Lysine is a well-researched antiviral amino acid. A lysine-containing complex has been shown to help maintain EBV latency. (Imai, et. al., 2014 as cited in Kines, 2018)

Probiotics- Probiotics help shift gut pH and support the intestinal immune system. One study showed that Lactobacillus acidophilus reversed exercise induced depletion of interferon gamma (IgA) secretion and subsequent control of EBV. (Clancy et. al., 2006)

Licorice- Licorice, or glycyrrhizic acid (GA) is the most powerful antiviral botanical available. (Kines, 2018) GA interferes with an early step of the EBV replication cycle. (Lin, 2003)

N-acetyl cysteine (NAC)- NAC, along with selenium, is one of Dr. Kines' favorite anti-EBV supplements. NAC is an NFkB modulator that also blocks viral replication. (Geiler, 2010 as cited in Kines, 2018)

Based on the evidence, EBV cannot thrive in an environment rich in antioxidants, fruits, vegetables, and nutrient dense unprocessed foods that are free of chemicals. With proven nutritional strategies, EBV can be kept in a harmless state. By incorporating specific foods and supplements and adjusting dosages according to whether they are in an acute active stage or a dormant stage, people with CAEBV can be more empowered to take control over their own health.

4 ROLE OF ENVIRONMENT

"24% of global disease is caused by environmental exposures that could be avoided." The World Health Organization

Environmental Toxins

Another factor affecting EBV is the environment in which we live. Unfortunately, there are many factors in our toxic world that can lead to reactivation of this virus. Every day we are exposed to chemicals in our food, water, and air, many of which are known carcinogens and completely unregulated. (Kristoff, 2010 as cited in Pizzorno, 2018). While diet and lifestyle play a significant role in health, symptoms of chronic disease often start with toxic overload. Toxic overload may come from any of the following: industrial toxins such as heavy metals; pollution and radiation released by industrial activities; agricultural toxins such as pesticides, hormones and herbicides; household toxins from building materials, rugs, paint and cleaning supplies; toxins in personal care products, perfumes and cosmetics; food toxins like genetically modified organisms (GMOs), food coloring, artificial flavors and artificial sweeteners; and other consumer product toxins like flame retardants in children's clothing, toys and blankets, non-stick cookware, and more. (Pizzorno, 2018) Additionally, we are poisoning ourselves with drugs, alcohol, and even the way we cook our food.

According to Dr. Joseph Pizzorno, author of *The Toxin Solution*, there are eight ways toxins damage our bodies: they poison enzymes, undermining bodily functions; they displace structural minerals; they damage organs and systems; they damage DNA; they modify gene expression, activating our genes in undesirable ways; they damage cell membranes so they don't respond properly; they interfere with hormones and cause imbalances; and they impair our ability to detoxify. While acute poisoning is rare, it's the chronic low-level exposure that's especially insidious. When our bodies accumulate high levels of toxins, they are stored in the brain, blood, and fat and interfere with essential bodily functions and processes. While the body has an innate capacity to detoxify itself, we were never meant to handle the level of toxins we are currently exposed to. "Toxins damage every aspect of our physiological function and play a role in virtually all diseases." (Pizzorno, 2018, p. 2)

There is a consensus in medical toxicology that environmental toxins affect the immune system and increase the risk of viral infections. (Kines, 2018) Epidemiological and animal studies implicate dioxins, cigarette smoke, diesel exhaust and other air pollutants. (Lawrence, 2007) Dioxins, one of the most dangerous manmade chemicals, are used in the production of pesticides. While dioxins are known to modulate the immune system, resulting in the development of autoimmune diseases, a 2012 study suggests a new role for dioxins as a pathogenic factor for autoimmune disease through EBV reactivation. In the study, 2, 3, 7, 8-tetrachlorodibenzo-p-dioxin (TCDD or dioxin) caused EBV reactivation in infected B cells in salivary gland epithelial cells, suggesting that this chemical is a risk factor for Sjogren's syndrome. (Inoue et. al., 2012) These observations indicate that pollutants are important but overlooked contributors to susceptibility and pathogenesis of viral infections.

Research now shows that allergies, immune impairment, autoimmune disease, degenerative neurological diseases, diabetes, and cancers that have become so common are due to nutrient deficiencies and an increasing toxic load. What makes connecting health problems to toxic load so challenging is that we are all physiologically unique. Each of us will have a somewhat different pattern of symptoms associated with specific toxins. Some people are more susceptible to immune system dysfunction, which will lead to allergies and autoimmune symptoms. Others might be more susceptible to mitochrondrial damage from toxins, so they'll tend to be more fatigued. (Pizzorno, 2018) Dr. Neil Nathan, MD, author of the book *Toxic*, says the three most common toxins that contribute to chronic illness appear to be molds, heavy metals (especially mercury), and pesticides (especially glyphosate). (Nathan, 2018) In addition, EBV creates it's own toxins as a byproduct of its metabolism. (Kines, 2018)

Heavy Metals

We are exposed to more mercury, lead, arsenic, cadmium, nickel, and aluminum today than most people realize, with mercury being one of the most common and dangerous metals to affect health. Because of the pollution of the oceans, large fish accumulate mercury. Frequent consumption of fish, even wild-caught salmon, can lead to high mercury levels. Although there is not direct research yet, heavy metals are thought to trigger reactivation of EBV. A current hypothesis suggests that viruses bind heavy metals stored in the body so efficiently that even chelating agents can't remove them and can only be removed from the body once the infection is gone. (Kines, 2018) Studies suggest that viruses have an affinity for mercury, so testing for heavy metals, especially mercury, may be helpful for those with CAEBV. (Yasko, 2004 as cited in Kines, 2018) Addressing heavy metal toxicity through natural chelating foods and supplements is imperative for those with CAEBV. Curcumin in turmeric is one such food that has the ability to remove heavy metals from the brain. (Kines, 2018) Chelation can be accomplished through other methods as well, but it can lead to intense detox symptoms so it's best to consult with a holistic health care professional with experience in this area.

Pesticides

Pesticide exposure is another common contributor to illness because the chemicals they contain are highly damaging to the immune, endocrine, and detoxification systems in the body. Glyphosate, known as Roundup, is the most common pesticide currently used on food crops, yards and public parks, making its way into our water. American commercial wheat is desiccated with glyphosate for harvesting, which may explain why 90% of the US population has detectable levels of glyphosate in their urine from ongoing exposure. Glyphosate kills the beneficial bacteria in the gut, leading to an array of disorders such as SIBO (Small Intestinal Bacterial Overgrowth) and research shows that it increases sensitivity to gluten. It's also been linked to Cancer. (Kines, 2018). Organophosphate pesticides are also widely used, and research suggests they may contribute to the reactivation of EBV and play an important role in the development of EBV-related diseases. (Zhao et. al., 2014) Many pesticides can't be completely detoxified by the body and accumulate in tissues. A study of people with CFS showed that they had much higher than average levels of organochloride pesticides in their red and white blood cells, which may have contributed their illness. (Dunstan, 1996) Reducing or eliminating conventional produce and factory farmed animal products and including organic foods in the diet will reduce exposure to these harmful toxins.

Mold

Mold toxicity is far more common than is currently recognized by medical practitioners, and the lack of scientific studies prevents them from being able to help patients suffering from it. Many of these toxins compromise the body's ability to detoxify, so they add to the body's toxic burden, especially for someone with reactivated EBV, since it makes it even more difficult to rid the body of the toxins created by the virus. These toxins directly poison the body's cells so they can no longer function as they should. (Nathan, 2018) Black mold is a huge problem because the chemicals and spores released by it disrupt the immune system and increase inflammation. (Pizzorno, 2018) By weakening the immune system, mold toxicity can be an invitation to the dormant virus to reactivate. Mold exposure includes not only current and direct exposure, but also exposure to mycotoxins made by mold, as well as to volatile organic compounds (VOC's) produced by it. Mycotoxins can directly impact immune regulation by causing an uncontrolled inflammatory release of cytokines. For those trying to heal, treating the virus when the primary problem is mold toxicity will not help the person heal. It's imperative to address mold toxicity before trying to treat EBV because mold toxicity makes recovering from EBV nearly impossible. (Nathan, 2018)

According to Dr. Klinghardt, M.D., Ph.D., one inch of black mold on a wall produced 20-40 mycotoxins in 24 hours, but when exposed to Electromagnetic Fields, (EMF), the mold produced 2000 in the same amount of time. Microbes exposed to EMF feel threatened and produce more toxins in self-defense. Studies suggest that EBV might also become more virulent when exposed to environmental toxins like mold as a self defense mechanism. This implication is an important consideration for those with CAEBV since these factors could make healing impossible. (Klinghardt, 2017)

Anyone who is not recovering with nutritional interventions should evaluate their home for mold and work on remediating the problem. However, because mold toxins can remain in the body for years, a past mold exposure could be contributing to current health issues. Dr. Nathan says that for most of his sickest patients, mold exposure happened years ago and may have colonized within their bodies to steadily produce mycotoxins on an ongoing basis. Fortunately, urine mycotoxin testing can easily confirm if someone has elevated levels of mycotoxins. (Nathan, 2018) Finding a mold literate physician or health care practitioner is extremely helpful, and following a mold detoxification program is essential for recovery.

Detoxification

With the massive amount of chemicals we're regularly exposed to in addition to the toxins produced when EBV is reactivated, detoxification is an essential part of regaining health. Knowing that environmental toxins affect immune function and increase the risk for EBV infection, it's important to support the body's detoxification organs on a regular basis as well. The liver is the major organ of detoxification, with the gastrointestinal tract, kidneys, lymphatic system, lungs, and skin also helping to move toxins out of the body. (Nathan, 2018) In order to effectively detox, the body's eliminatory organs must be functioning optimally. Chronic infections like CAEBV take a toll on the liver, so supporting the liver with nutrient dense food is important. Eating organic produce will reduce the body's toxic burden, and clean animal proteins, including whey protein can help support detoxification. Beets and leafy greens, especially dandelion, have a long-standing reputation for providing liver support. In addition, a diet with adequate fiber will ensure proper motility of the digestive tract to aid in the elimination of toxins. It's also important to get enough sleep, especially between the hours of 10:30pm and 2:30am, as this is the time for daily repair. Being asleep at this time ensures the liver detoxifies and the body and brain get needed repair. (Kines, 2018)

Water is an extremely important factor for detoxification, as it helps flush toxins from the body. Water also helps maintain alkalinity in our blood, lymph, and intracellular fluids by diluting excess acidity from cellular metabolism, acidic food, lifestyle, and thoughts. (Young, 2001) Therefore, the quality of water we drink is just as important as the quality of our food. Because most tap water today is contaminated with industrial chemicals, pesticides, heavy metals and pharmaceutical drug residues as well as added chlorine and fluoride, finding a source of filtered water is necessary. Investing in a reverse osmosis or distillation system ensures pure water is available at all times. Using a shower filter will also minimize toxic exposure since the skin absorbs a large percentage of chemicals directly into the bloodstream without the benefit of being filtered by the liver.

The lymphatic system is also crucial for regular detoxification and immune function because it helps remove toxins from the body as well as the toxic debris left behind by EBV. This system contains 600 lymph nodes where toxins and viral cells are collected before removal. Swollen lymph nodes in the neck are often the first sign of an EBV reactivation since the virus is attacking B and T cells there. (Kines, 2018) If lymph gets blocked, immune function weakens and we are susceptible to pathogens. Since the lymphatic system relies on movement, a sedentary lifestyle contributes to stagnation of lymph, buildup of toxins, and poor immune function. Walking, hopping, bouncing on a trampoline, jumping rope, or running all stimulate the flow of lymph. Yoga, lymphatic massage, dry brushing, and even deep breathing also help stimulate this system.

Sweating is another important way to help rid the body of toxins. The skin is the largest elimination organ and many toxins are released with sweat. Epsom salt baths are one way to induce sweating, as well as increase magnesium levels and help detoxification and relaxation. (Nathan, 2018)

Saunas can induce sweating and enhance mobilization of fat-soluble toxins. A sauna is one of the few ways than can help the body excrete dangerous "persistent organic pollutants" that are hard to rid the body of. They also enhance mobilization of heavy metals, BPA, and xenobiotics. Far Infrared Saunas are especially helpful for moving toxins from fat tissues into the bloodstream to be eliminated through the liver. (Kines, 2018) Not only that, but acute heat stress can enhance immune function. (Cohen et al., 2020) In addition, studies suggest that repeated sauna therapy can reduce oxidative stress. (Masuda et. al., 2004)

Electromagnetic Fields

Exposure to electromagnetic fields (EMF) is another potential reactivating factor for EBV. Today we are exposed to amounts and types of radiation never before encountered in the history of mankind. In his book *The Invisible Rainbow*, Arthur Firstenberg points out the correlation between flu pandemics with rapid changes in the earth's electromagnetic environment. From power lines ushering in the 1889 flu pandemic, followed by the Spanish flu pandemic of 1918 with the advent of the radio era, the Asian flu pandemic of 1957 with the beginning of the radar era, and the Hong Kong flu pandemic of 1968 when the satellite era began, viral outbreaks appear to coincide with these shifts. More recently, the beginning of the wireless era coincided with the collapse of Europe's honeybee population, and the activation of the High Frequency Active Auroral Research Program (HAARP), the most powerful radio transmitter on earth, is thought to be responsible for the worldwide outbreak of Colony Collapse Disorder. (Firstenberg, 2020)

This brings up an important and often overlooked aspect to health: that electromagnetic radiation affects biological systems. According to Dr. Lipton, hundreds of scientific studies over the last fifty years have revealed that the electromagnetic spectrum profoundly impacts every part of biological regulation. Specific frequencies of electromagnetic radiation regulate DNA, RNA, and protein synthesis, alter protein shape and function, and control gene regulation along with many other fundamental processes. Though these studies have been published in some of the most respected biomedical journals, their findings haven't made their way into the medical school curriculum. (Lipton, 2015) A 1997 study exposing EBV cells to an electromagnetic field of just 50 Hz in latently infected human lymphoid cells resulted in an increased number of cells expressing EBV early antigens. This finding provides evidence that EBV can be modulated by a magnetic field. (Grimaldi, et. al., 1997) In testing, positive early antigen antibodies indicate an active or reactivated infection. Considering that a traditional wired desktop computer emits 60-100 Hz and wireless connections emit 10 MHz to 300 GHz, this is cause for concern. Since our daily exposure to EMF is much higher than the 50 Hz in the study, being continuously exposed may perpetuate EBV infection. (Kines, 2018)

The use of cell phones is also a potential trigger for EBV reactivation. The World Health Organization admits that cell phone radiation may be linked to brain cancer, and several countries have issued warnings to reduce cell phone exposure. (Kines, 2018) The EBV early antigen (EBV-EA) can be expressed when certain cells are stimulated by chemical or physical carcinogens. A 2013 study investigated the role of cell phones and found that cell phone radiation could induce the expression of EBV-EA. (Yiang, L. et. al., 2013)

EMF's from television, radio, microwaves, cell phones, cell towers, radio transmitters, wireless routers, and smart meters installed on homes are unavoidable. Dr. Kines says that EMF from smart meters is a potential danger to anyone with EBV since they pulse on and off around the clock. Smart meters have been compared to being 200-600 feet away from a cell tower. They give off RF radiation, which is classified by the International Agency for Research on Cancer (IARC) as "possibly carcinogenic to humans." (Kines, 2018) Considering the risks, anyone with CAEBV should be aware of their daily EMF exposure and do what they can to minimize it. Perhaps the most important step to take is to have the smart meter removed or at least install a protective shield over it. Most companies will replace a smart meter with an analogue meter for a monthly fee that is well worth the cost.

Other ways to reduce EMF exposure include keeping electronics out of the bedroom and turning Wifi off at night to give the body a break from the constant barrage of radiation. Using wired headsets or speaker mode instead of blue tooth headsets, holding the phone away from the body, avoiding use of the phone while in a car, only making calls when the signal is strong, texting instead of talking can minimize EMF exposure from cell phones. (EWG) A 2001 health survey published in International Journal of Hygiene and Environmental Health determined that removing or disconnecting indoor EMF sources was the most effective action for those who had experienced symptoms attributed to EMF exposure. (Roosli, et al., 2004) Recent studies on mice suggest that antioxidants may play an important role in counteracting the effects of radiation. One study showed that rosemary extract could play a protective role against the harmful effects of EMF through its antioxidant activity. (Ghoneim and Arafat, 2016) Another study on mice exposed to gamma radiation demonstrated the radio-protective effect of rosemary extract. (Jindal et. al., 2006)

Since the electromagnetic fields that surround us hold a positive charge, we are immersed in positive ions that are associated with inflammation, depression, anxiety, and chronic disease. In addition, stress induced inflammatory cytokines, as well as free radicals and oxidation are also positively charged. Oxidation has been shown in studies to increase the risk of EBV reactivation, but negative ions act as free radical scavengers. (Kines, 2018) The Earth has freely available negative ions that are beneficial and necessary to balance the human body. Research suggests that disconnection from the Earth's negative ions may be a major contributor to physiological dysfunction, and studies have shown that direct physical contact with the Earth's surface has a surprisingly beneficial effect on human health. According to one study, going barefoot for as little as 30-40 minutes a day can significantly reduce pain and stress. (Ober et. al., 2010) Another study suggests that contact with the Earth- whether from going barefoot outside or using grounded conductive systems indoors, can have a profound effect on health issues like pain, inflammation, and stress. The research shows that grounding the human body may be an essential part in the health equation along with sunshine, clean air and water, nutritious food and physical activity. (Chevalier et. al., 2012)

5 ROLE OF STRESS

"If you ask what is the single most important key to longevity, I would have to say it is avoiding worry, stress, and tension. And if you didn't ask me, I'd still have to say it." George Burns

Stress comes in many forms and can be an even greater contributing factor for EBV reactivation than anything else. Dr. Lisa Rankin, author of *Mind over Medicine*, says that based on her experience with patients, she believes that whether patients get sick or stay healthy, whether they stay sick or heal, may have more to do with everything else going on in the person's life than with any healthy thing they do. (Rankin, 2013) Someone can eat a perfectly clean, organic diet yet be overwhelmed with stress or even just toxic thoughts and end up with a reactivation of EBV. That's because the release of stress hormones contributes to an acidic, oxygen-deprived environment within the body, creating an ideal condition for the virus to thrive. Dr. Young found through his research that cellular disturbance can be caused by physical, emotional, and/or spiritual stress. (Young, 2001) Considering so many "health nuts" are in poor health, perhaps it is because they are forgetting a big part of the health equation.

When we experience stress, the sympathetic nervous system is activated. The HPA axis (Hypothalamus-Pituitary-Adrenal axis) prepares the body for fight or flight by stimulating the release of cortisol and adrenaline to help us either fight off an attacker or run away. When the threat passes, activation of the HPA axis should dissipate and our nervous system should return to a state of parasympathetic dominance. This system works great in an emergency, but was not intended to be activated continuously. The problem today is that most people are under a tremendous amount of chronic stress and instead of the HPA axis being activated periodically when needed, they are living in a state of chronic sympathetic nervous system dominance. When we are in fight or flight mode, immune function is suppressed. (Lipton, 2015)

When we are relaxed, the parasympathetic nervous system is in charge. This system is associated with the vagus nerve, which runs from the brainstem to the abdomen and regulates many bodily functions necessary for maintaining homeostasis. When the brain perceives safety, the hypothalamus stops triggering the stress response, vagal tone increases, which shuts off the sympathetic nervous system, and cortisol and adrenaline levels drop. Once the body is back in a state of parasympathetic dominance, the immune system turns back on and the body's self repair processes can do their job. (Rosenberg, 2017) In a state of parasympathetic dominance, disease is less likely in well people and may even be healed in sick people. (Rankin, 2013)

Reactivation of EBV typically follows stressful or traumatic events. Periods of intense stress, such as loss of a loved one, attending college, or even loneliness, have been shown to increase EBV antibodies in latent cases. (Kiecolt-Glaser, 1984) Even life changing events that are positive, like buying a home, getting married, or starting a new job can add to a person's stress load. The number one reactivating factor Dr. Kines sees in her practice is extreme or compounding negative stress. "Lack of sleep, chronic inflammation, overmedication, poor diet, surgeries, overwork, and overcommitting are all stressors, regardless of your emotional state, but still, emotional stressors can be the most devastating and the biggest reactivators, hands down." (Kines, 2018, p. 43)

Emotional Stress

Taking care of the physical body while neglecting emotional issues is not a recipe for health because emotions are capable of shifting the body's chemistry. Emotional toxicity can be just as harmful as toxins in our environment. Research shows that negative beliefs may affect the body by triggering the stress response, shutting down the body's self-repair mechanisms and setting us up for disease. (Chida and Steptoe as cited in

Rankin, 2013) Research has confirmed that brain cells translate the mind's beliefs into complementary and unique chemical profiles that control the body's cells. Thoughts directly influence how the brain controls the body's physiology. (Lipton, 2015) Our thoughts, beliefs, feelings, and traumas influence the autonomic nervous system. Fear, anger, frustration, and resentment trigger the stress response. (Dienstbier, 1989 as cited in Rankin, 2013) It doesn't matter if we're not in real danger. What matters is that our mind believes we are and in turn, releases cortisol, which suppresses immune function. (Lipton, 2015) "To an extent that immunologists and psychologists rarely appreciate, we are architects of our own experience. Your subjective experience carries more power than your objective situation," says Steve Cole- epigeneticist at UCLA's School of Medicine. (Lipton, 2015, p. 147) Our physical body reflects the state of our mental, emotional, and spiritual health. Even scientific data suggests that a healthy mind and a connection with a spiritual life may be equally, if not more important to the health of the body. (Rankin, 2013)

"What is the impact of the fear (emotional toxicity) that the word 'virus' brings to mind and heart?" (Young, 2001, p. 251) According to Dr. Young, the fear of viruses is a fundamental error of the germ theory, and can be responsible for creating sickness through the power of auto-suggestion. "Ironically, if the germ theory were founded on facts it would be correct to fear viruses, except there would be few, if any, humans living to discuss the issues," says Young. (2001, p. 251) According to Lipton, learning to harness the mind to promote growth is the secret of life. We can choose to believe in a world full of fear, shutting down our body's protection response. Or we can choose to see a world full of love and allow our body to respond by growing in health. (Lipton, 2015) Belief is a more powerful healing mechanism than most people realize. Take the example of AIDS patients in Africa, who were dying from the disease but when they were tested and found to be negative, they suddenly rebounded and became healthy. (Bleker, 1993 as cited in Young, 2001)

Chronic adversity or trauma in childhood is another form of emotional stress that is known to change the way our genes are expressed. Undergoing chronic stressful conditions can directly impact how genes are expressed. With the Polyvagal Theory, Stephen Porges, Ph.D. expanded our knowledge of how the vagus nerve influences health. He acknowledged that there are two branches of the vagus nerve, one of which is more primitive. If a person experiences chronic, ongoing trauma, the more primitive branch can be stimulated and instead of the fight of flight response being activated, the freeze response takes over. As the body becomes more accustomed to the stress response and the more primitive branch of the vagus nerve is in charge, the person essentially becomes "frozen," which impacts physical, mental, and emotional health. (Rosenberg, 2017)

It is clear that addressing unresolved emotions and traumas is a necessary factor in healing. It's important to be mindful of our self-talk. If someone with CAEBV continually tells himself that he's sick, the body will respond by being sick. While it's important to know what we're dealing with, it's not helpful to allow a label to define us. Identifying with a disease can actually be detrimental, as it may create a self-fulfilling prophecy. In the words of philosopher Ralph Waldo Trine, "Never affirm or repeat about your health what you do not wish to be true." (Rankin, 2013, p. 23)

Physiological Stress

Stress isn't just an emotional burden we are aware of. Lack of sunlight; changes in circadian rhythm; hormonal changes such as puberty, menopause, or postpartum; exams; lack of physical space; and loneliness all cause physiological stress on the body. (Kines, 2018) According to Steve Cole, "If you actually measure stress using our best available instruments, it can't hold a candle to social isolation. Social isolation is the best-established, most robust social or psychological risk factor for disease out there. Nothing can compete." (Lipton, 2015, p. 140)

A common source of physiological stress is exercise. While important for staying healthy and reducing stress, exercise can be detrimental if it's too much or too intense, as it creates oxidative stress. Research has shown that lack of exercise increases the risk of infection, while moderate exercise reduces infection risk. Innumerable studies show that by helping to coordinate the pattern of methylation and gene expression, exercise is one of the most powerful ways to enhance immunity and avoid disease. (Vasquez, 2014) While exercise is important, overdoing it in the gym or running long distances can be a trigger for viral reactivation. A study on over-trained athletes showed that "intense exercise and overtraining create high levels of oxidation (and thus free radical damage)." (Kines, 2018, p. 97) The increase in infections following extreme exercise such as marathons appears to be related to oxidative stress, release of the stress hormone cortisol, and antioxidant depletion. (Vasquez, 2014) An animal study showed that moderate exercise reduces the risk of infection by modulating the immune system, reducing excess inflammation, and promoting lymphatic flow, which is critical for immune function. (Knott et al., 2005, as cited in Vasquez, 2014) One study found that increased shedding of EBV was associated with intense training in elite athletes. (Clancy, et. al., 2006)

Relationships are another important and often unappreciated factor in health. "While loneliness, anger, and resentment evoke the poisonous biochemistry of threat reactions, the desire for connection, intimacy, and a sense of belonging with family, lovers, and friends is hardwired in our DNA, and when these desires are fulfilled, our bodies respond with better health." (Rankin, 2013, p. 85) The impact of relationships, especially a spousal relationship, cannot be underestimated when it comes to health. "Relationships can be medicine or poison." (Rankin, 2013, p. 103) An unhappy relationship can be dangerous for our health because it can frequently activate the stress response. An Ohio University study published in the journal *Cancer*, which examined 100 patients with breast cancer, showed that those in bad marriages fared less well than those in happy marriages. (Ohio, 2008 as cited in Rankin, 2013) Another study suggests that in a healthy relationship, holding our partner's hand is enough to lower blood pressure, ease stress responses, improve health, and diminish pain. (Coan et al., 2006) Feeling loved and supported in a relationship activates the relaxation response that is key to staying healthy. "Love opens your heart, trumps fear, and paves the way for healing in all aspects of your life." (Rankin, 2013, p. 88)

Minimizing Stress to Positively affect Health

Identifying and reducing the causes of stress is one of the most important things someone can do to heal from CAEBV. Whether it's spending time in nature, journaling, or spending time with loved ones, calming the stress response will increase the chance for healing. Spending time in the sun provides an added health bonus because exposing our skin to the sun allows us to make vitamin D. In addition, researchers at Georgetown University Medical Center have found that sunlight energizes T cells that play a major role in immune function. (Sunlight offers surprise, 2016) The practice of writing in a gratitude journal is a way to induce the relaxation response and has been shown to keep people optimistic or help develop an optimistic attitude, which will increase the chancing of healing. (Kines, 2018) Even laughter can have a powerful effect on healing. After being diagnosed with a serious degenerative disorder, Norman Cousins, author of Anatomy of an Illness, checked himself out of the hospital and replaced the anti-inflammatory drugs, painkillers, and tranquilizers with high doses of vitamin C and daily laughter from watching funny shows. (Rankin, 2013) His story also demonstrates the amazing healing power of the mind. He believed the hospital was not conducive to his healing and that he would be able to heal if he was in the right environment, and he did.

Practicing mindfulness is a proven way to activate the parasympathetic nervous system. It involves focusing on the breath, thoughts, and bodily sensations while seated, walking, or practicing yoga. Research suggests that mindfulness meditation may relieve chronic inflammation. ("People suffering from", 2013) Walking, washing dishes, mowing the lawn, and cooking can all be forms of meditation if the activity is done with awareness. The health benefits of meditation have been well documented. One groundbreaking study documented that the relaxation response induced by practices like yoga, mediation, deep breathing, and prayer produces immediate changes in the expression of genes involved in immune function, energy metabolism, and insulin secretion. (Bhasin, et al., 2013 as cited in Lipton, 2005) Meditation decreases stress-related cortisol, reduces respiration and heart rate, reduces metabolic rate, increases blood flow in the brain, strengthens the immune system, leads to a state of relaxation, and activates neural changes in the brain. (Davidson et.al., 2003 as cited in Rankin, 2013). Deep breathing exercises will also calm the stress response. Stress causes people to shallow breath or even hold their breath, which causes respiratory acidosis, and deep breathing is the easiest way to correct it. (Young, 2001)

It is clear that stress in all forms can be extremely detrimental to our health. Evidence shows that minimizing stress and activating the parasympathetic nervous system has profound benefits for our emotional, spiritual, and physical health. When we are mindful of our stressors and tune in to what our bodies are telling us, we can bring ourselves into balance, which will provide the opportunity to heal from CAEBV and experience vibrant health. In her popular 2011 TEDx talk, "The Truth about Your Health," Dr. Rankin introduced her Whole Health Cairn, a wellness model she created after being inspired by a stack of balanced stones she saw marking a hiking trail. She calls the foundation stone, the one upon which everything else is built, the "Inner Pilot Light" that she describes as "that inner knowing, the healing wisdom of your body and soul that knows what's true for you and guides you, in your own unique way, back to better health." While most wellness models teach that the body is the foundation, we've gotten it backward. "The body is the physical manifestation of the sum of your life experiences. When your life is out of alignment with your Inner Pilot Light and the stones of your Whole Health Cairn are out of balance, your nervous system kicks into stress response, and your body suffers." (2013, p. 87) Fortunately, this is all within our control. By developing a greater awareness of our thoughts, our emotions, and our language, we can learn how to change course when needed and harness our bodies' own healing capacity.

6 CONCLUSION

Germs are everywhere. They exist all around us and inside of us. Will the scientific community ever study what actually makes them pathological? It seems unlikely when much of science is closely tied to the pharmaceutical industry and when the solution involves choices that are within the individual's control. After all, there isn't much profit in wellness. In the future, will the medical community see viruses as serving a necessary purpose in the body in the same way bacteria in the digestive tract serve a necessary and life-sustaining purpose, as Antoine Bechamp suggested? Only time will tell. Regardless, the focus should be on keeping the terrain healthy to ensure EBV is kept in a harmless state.

It is clear that mainstream medicine is not well equipped to deal with chronic illnesses like CAEBV. With symptom management as their only answer, patients too often end up confused and in worse health as the result of ignoring the root cause of illness and adding to the body's dysfunction and toxic burden through the use of pharmaceuticals. Despite the fact that mainstream medicine doesn't recognize EBV as an underlying factor in many of today's chronic illnesses, there is plenty of research linking the virus to many ailments. More importantly, there is also plenty of evidence that the virus can be kept in a dormant state with natural methods. Knowing what triggers reactivation and using nutritional and lifestyle interventions can empower those with EBV to reclaim their health by bringing the body, mind, and soul back into harmony.

Science may continue to look for genetic clues as to why this virus often leads to serious diseases, but we know that genetics plays a small role and that nutrient status, environment, and lifestyle have a greater influence in whether the virus becomes pathological or not. While science continues to dive deeper into a rabbit hole with seemingly no end, we can focus on the power we have been given by our Creator to heal when we provide our bodies with what they need to do so. It's time to change the dismal medical perspective for EBV and recognize that there are proven strategies for keeping the virus in check and eliminating viral related chronic illness.

BIBLIOGRAPHY

Balch, P. (2010) *Prescription for nutritional healing: a practical a-to-z reference to drug-free remedies using vitamins, minerals, herbs, and food supplements.* New York, NY: The Penguin Group.

Beard, J. A., Bearden, A., & Striker, R. (2011). Vitamin D and the anti-viral state. *Journal of clinical virology : the official publication of the Pan American Society for Clinical Virology, 50*(3), 194–200. https://doi.org/10.1016/j.jcv.2010.12.006

Batt, R. (2016, June 16) I've got the cookie. [Blog post] Retrieved from https://renabatt.wordpress.com/tag/dr-arthur-c-guyton/

Carnahan, J., M.D. The Sleeping Giant- Tips to Treat Reactivation of Epstein-Barr Virus. https://www.jillcarnahan.com/2018/01/25/sleeping-giant-tips-treat-reactivation-epstein-barr-virus/

CDC. (2020) Epstein-Barr Virus and Infectious Mononucleosis. Retrieved from https://www.cdc.gov/epstein-barr/index.html

Chang LK, Wei TT, Chiu YF, Tung CP, Chuang JY, Hung SK, Li C, Liu ST. Inhibition of Epstein-Barr virus lytic cycle by (-)-epigallocatechin gallate. Biochem Biophys Res Commun. 2003 Feb 21;301(4):1062-8. doi: 10.1016/s0006-291x(03)00067-6. PMID: 12589821.

Chen C, Reddy KS, Johnston TD, Khan TT, Ranjan D. Vitamin E inhibits cyclosporin A and H2O2 promoted Epstein-Barr virus (EBV) transformation of human B cells as assayed by EBV oncogene LMP1 expression. J Surg Res. 2003 Aug;113(2):228-33. doi:

10.1016/s0022-4804(03)00187-2. PMID: 12957134.

Clancy RL, Gleeson M, Cox A, Callister R, Dorrington M, D'Este C, Pang G, Pyne D, Fricker P, & Henriksson A. Reversal in fatigued athletes of a defect in interferon gamma secretion after administration of Lactobacillus acidophilus. Br J Sports Med. 2006 Apr;40(4):351-4. doi: 10.1136/bjsm.2005.024364. PMID: 16556792; PMCID: PMC2577537.

Chevalier, G., Sinatra, S. T., Oschman, J. L., Sokal, K., & Sokal, P. (2012). Earthing: health implications of reconnecting the human body to the Earth's surface electrons. *Journal of environmental and public health, 2012*, 291541. https://doi.org/10.1155/2012/291541

Cohen, J. I., Jaffe, E. S., Dale, J. K., Pittaluga, S., Heslop, H. E., Rooney, C. M., Gottschalk, S., Bollard, C. M., Rao, V. K., Marques, A., Burbelo, P. D., Turk, S. P., Fulton, R., Wayne, A. S., Little, R. F., Cairo, M. S., El-Mallawany, N. K., Fowler, D., Sportes, C., Bishop, M. R., ... Straus, S. E. (2011). Characterization and treatment of chronic active Epstein-Barr virus disease: a 28-year experience in the United States. *Blood, 117*(22), 5835–5849. https://doi.org/10.1182/blood-2010-11-316745

Coan, J. A., Schaefer, H. S., & Davidson, R. J. (2006). Lending a hand: social regulation of the neural response to threat. *Psychological science, 17*(12), 1032–1039. https://doi.org/10.1111/j.1467-9280.2006.01832.x

Cohen, J. I. (2009). Optimal treatment for chronic active Epstein-Barr virus disease. *Pediatric transplantation, 13*(4), 393–396. https://doi.org/10.1111/j.1399-3046.2008.01095.x

Cohen, M. (2020). Turning up the heat on COVID-19: heat as a therapeutic intervention. *F1000Research, 9*, 292. https://doi.org/10.12688/f1000research.232

Crawford, D. H., Rickinson, A., & Johannessen, I. (2014) *Cancer virus: the story of epstein-barr virus.* New York, NY: Oxford University Press.

Crinnion, WJ. Organic foods contain higher levels of certain nutrients, lower levels of pesticides, and may provide health benefits for the consumer. Altern Med Rev. 2010 Apr;15(1):4-12. PMID: 20359265.

De Paschale, M., & Clerici, P. (2012). Serological diagnosis of Epstein-Barr virus infection: Problems and solutions. *World journal of virology*, *1*(1), 31–43. https://doi.org/10.5501/wjv.v1.i1.31

Dinarello, CA *(August 2000). "Proinflammatory cytokines". Chest.* ***118*** *(2): 503–8. doi:10.1378/chest.118.2.503. PMID 10936147*

Dunstan, R. H., et al., Chlorinated hydrocarbon and chronic fatigue syndrome. Med J Aust, 1996. 164 (4): p. 251.

Eligio, P., Delia, R., & Valeria, G. (2010). EBV Chronic Infections. *Mediterranean journal of hematology and infectious diseases*, *2*(1), e2010022. https://doi.org/10.4084/MJHID.2010.022

EWG's Guide to Safer Cell Phone Use. Retrieved September 15, 2020, from https://www.ewg.org/research/cellphone-radiation

Firstenberg, A. (2020) *The invisible rainbow: a history of electricity and life.* White River Junction, VT: Chelsea Green Publishing.

Flavin, D. (2006) Reversing Splenomegalies in Epstein Barr Virus Infected Children: Mechanisms of Toxicity in Viral Diseases. Journal of Orthomolecular Medicine, 21. https://www.researchgate.net/publication/242615980_Reversing_Splenomegalies_in_Epstein_Barr_Virus_Infected_Children_Mechanisms_of_Toxicity_in_Viral_Diseases

Ghoneim F & Afafat, E. Histological and histochemical study of the protective role of rosemary extract against harmful effect of cell phone electromagnetic radiation on the parotid glands. Acta Histochemica. June 2016; Volume 118, Issue 5, pgs. 478-485. Retrieved from https://www.sciencedirect.com/science/article/abs/pii/S0065128116300678

Grimaldi S, Pasquali E, Barbatano L, Lisi A, Santoro N, Serafino & A, Pozzi D. Exposure to a 50 Hz electromagnetic field induces activation of the Epstein-Barr virus genome in latently infected human lymphoid cells. J Environ Pathol Toxicol Oncol. 1997;16(2-3):205-7. PMID: 9276003.

Inoue, H., Mishima, K.,Yamamoto-Yoshida, S., Ushikoshi-Nakayama, R., Nakagawa, Y., Yamamoto, K., Ryo, K., Ide, F., & Saito, I. Aryl Hydrocarbon Receptor-Mediated Induction of EBV Reactivation as a Risk Factor for Sjögren's Syndrome

Iwase Y, Takemura Y, Ju-ichi M, Kawaii S, Yano M, Okuda Y, Mukainaka T, Tsuruta A, Okuda M, Takayasu J, Tokuda H, & Nishino H. Inhibitory effect of Epstein-Barr virus activation by Citrus fruits, a cancer chemopreventor. Cancer Lett. 1999 May 24;139(2):227-36. doi: 10.1016/s0304-3835(99)00041-5. PMID: 10395183.

Janegova, A., Janega, P., Rychly, B., Kuracinova, K., & Babal, P. (2015). The role of Epstein-Barr virus infection in the development of autoimmune thyroid diseases. *Endokrynologia Polska*, *66*(2), 132–136. https://doi.org/10.5603/EP.2015.0020

Jian SW, Mei CE, Liang YN, Li D, Chen QL, Luo HL, Li YQ, & Cai TY. [Influence of selenium-rich rice on transformation of umbilical blood B lymphocytes by Epstein-Barr virus and Epstein-Barr virus early antigen expression]. Ai Zheng. 2003 Jan;22(1):26-9. Chinese. PMID: 12561431.

Jindal A, Soyal D, Sancheti G, & Goyal PK. Radioprotective potential of Rosemarinus officinalis against lethal effects of gamma radiation : a preliminary study. J Environ Pathol Toxicol Oncol. 2006;25(4):633-42. doi: 10.1615/jenvironpatholtoxicoloncol.v25.i4.30. PMID: 17341204.

Kawamoto, K., Miyoshi, H., Suzuki, T., Kozai, Y., Kato, K., Miyahara, M., Yujiri, T., Choi, I., Fujimaki, K., Muta, T., Kume, M., Moriguchi, S., Tamura, S., Kato, T., Tagawa, H., Makiyama, J., Kanisawa, Y., Sasaki, Y., Kurita, D., Yamada, K., … Ohshima, K. (2018). A distinct subtype of Epstein-Barr virus-positive T/NK-cell lymphoproliferative disorder: adult patients with chronic active Epstein-Barr virus infection-like features. *Haematologica, 103*(6), 1018–1028. https://doi.org/10.3324/haematol.2017.174177

Kerr JR. (2019) Epstein-Barr virus (EBV) reactivation and therapeutic inhibitors. Journal of Clinical Pathology;72:651-658.

Kiecolt-Glaser JK, Speicher CE, Holliday JE, & Glaser R. Stress and the transformation of lymphocytes by Epstein-Barr virus. J Behav Med. 1984 Mar;7(1):1-12. doi: 10.1007/BF00845344. PMID: 6325704.

Kines, K. (2018) *The Epstein-barr virus solution: the hidden undiagnosed epidemic of a virus destroying millions of lives through chronic fatigue, autoimmune disorders, and cancer.* Columbia, SC.

Kimura, H. & Cohen, J.I.. (2017, December 22) Chronic Active Epstein-Barr Virus Disease. Front. Immunol. | https://doi.org/10.3389/fimmu.2017.01867

Klinghardt, D. (2017) EMF and the Potentiation of Pathogens and Heavy Metals: Effective Mitigation and Detox. Theklinghardtinstitute.com. Retrieved from https://aonm.org/wp-content/uploads/2017/11/Dr.-Klinghardt-EMF-and-the-Potentiation-of-Pathogens-and-Heavy-Metals.pdf

Lin JC. Mechanism of action of glycyrrhizic acid in inhibition of Epstein-Barr virus replication in vitro. Antiviral Res. 2003 Jun;59(1):41-7. doi: 10.1016/s0166-3542(03)00030-5. PMID: 12834859.

Lawrence, BP. Environmental toxins as modulators of antiviral immune responses. Viral Immunol. 2007 Summer;20(2):231-42. doi: 10.1089/vim.2007.0013. PMID: 17603840.

Lipton, B. H. (2015) *The biology of belief: Unleashing the power of consciousness, matter and miracles.* Carlsbad, CA: Hay House, Inc.

Masuda, A., Miyata, M., Kihara, T., Minagoe, S., & Tei, C. (2004). Repeated sauna therapy reduces urinary 8-epi-prostaglandin

F(2alpha). *Japanese heart journal, 45*(2), 297–303. https://doi.org/10.1536/jhj.45.297

Merriam-Webster.com. Merriam-Webster.com Medical Dictionary. Retrieved September 7, 2020, from https://www.merriam-webster.com/medical/lymphotropic

Mindfulness meditation may relieve chronic inflammation. University of Wisconsin-Madison. (2013, January 16). *ScienceDaily.* Retrieved October 22, 2020 from www.sciencedaily.com/releases/2013/01/130116163536.htm

Miyamura T, Chayama K, Wada T, Yamaguchi K, Yamashita N, Ishida T, Washio K, Morishita N, Manki A, Oda M, & Morishima T. Two cases of chronic active Epstein-Barr virus infection in which EBV-specific cytotoxic T lymphocyte was induced after allogeneic bone marrow transplantation. Pediatr Transplant. 2008 Aug;12(5):588-92. doi: 10.1111/j.1399-3046.2007.00873.x. Epub 2008 Feb 6. PMID: 18266798.

Nathan, N. (2018) *Toxic: heal your body from mold toxicity, lyme disease, multiple chemical sensitivities, and chronic environmental illness.* Las Vegas, NV: Victory Belt Publishing.

National Institute of Health. Chronic active Epstein-barr virus infection. Retrieved September 28, 2020, from https://rarediseases.info.nih.gov/diseases/9534/chronic-active-epstein-barr-virus-infection

Ober C, Sinatra ST, & Zucker M. *Earthing: The Most Important Health Discovery Ever?* Laguna Beach, Calif, USA: Basic Health Publications; 2010. [Google Scholar]

Pender, M. P. "CD8+ T-Cell Deficiency, Epstein-Barr Virus Infection, Vitamin D Deficiency, and Steps to Autoimmunity: A Unifying Hypothesis", *Autoimmune Diseases*, vol. 2012, Article ID 189096, 16 pages, 2012. https://doi.org/10.1155/2012/189096

Pizzorno, J. E. (2018). *The toxin solution: how hidden poisons in the air, water, food, and products we use are destroying our health--and what we can do to fix it.* New York, NY: Harper One.

Pozzi, D., Faggioni, A., Zompetta, C., De Ros, I., Lio, S., Lisi, A., Ravagnan, G., Frati, L., & Grimaldi, S. (1992). Charge and pH effect on the early events of Epstein-Barr virus fusion with lymphoblastoid cells (Raji). *Intervirology, 33*(4), 173-179. https://doi.org/10.1159/000150248

Rankin, L M.D. (2013). *Mind over medicine: scientific proof that you can heal yourself.* Carlsbad, CA: Hay House, Inc.

Romm, A. Epstein-Barr Virus (EBV), Fatigue, and Hashimoto's: Breaking the Cycle Naturally. Retrieved September 28, 2020, from https://avivaromm.com/ebv-thyroid-connection/

Röösli M, Moser M, Baldinini Y, Meier M, Braun-Fahrländer C. Symptoms of ill health ascribed to electromagnetic field exposure--a questionnaire survey. Int J Hyg Environ Health. 2004 Feb;207(2):141-50. doi: 10.1078/1438-4639-00269. PMID: 15031956.

Rosenberg, Stanley. (2017). *Accessing the healing power of the vagus nerve.* Berkeley, CA: North Atlantic Books.

Røsjø E, Lossius A, Abdelmagid N, et al. Effect of high-dose vitamin D3 supplementation on antibody responses against Epstein–Barr virus in relapsing-remitting multiple sclerosis. Multiple Sclerosis Journal. 2017;23(3):395-402. doi:10.1177/1352458516654310

Shannon-Lowe, C., & Rickinson, A. (2019). The Global Landscape of EBV-Associated Tumors. *Frontiers in oncology, 9*, 713. https://doi.org/10.3389/fonc.2019.00713

Smatti, M. K., Al-Sadeq, D. W., Ali, N. H., Pintus, G., Abou-Saleh, H., & Nasrallah, G. K. (2018). Epstein-Barr Virus Epidemiology, Serology, and Genetic Variability of LMP-1 Oncogene Among Healthy Population: An Update. *Frontiers in oncology, 8*, 211. https://doi.org/10.3389/fonc.2018.00211

Sunlight offers surprise benefit: It energizes infection fighting T cells. Georgetown University Medical Center. (2016, December 20). *ScienceDaily*. Retrieved October 14, 2020 from www.sciencedaily.com/releases/2016/12/161220094633.htm

Tarlinton, R. E., Martynova, E., Rizvanov, A. A., Khaiboullina, S., & Verma, S. (2020). Role of Viruses in the Pathogenesis of Multiple Sclerosis. *Viruses, 12*(6), 643. https://doi.org/10.3390/v12060643

Vasquez, A. (2014) *Antiviral Strategies and Immune Nutrition against colds, flu, herpes, aids, hepatitis, ebola, dengue, and autoimmunity: a concept-based and evidence-based handbook and research review for practical use.* Columbia, SC.

Weber, N. D., Andersen, D. O., North, J. A., Murray, B. K., Lawson, L. D., & Hughes, B. G. (1992). In vitro virucidal effects of Allium sativum (garlic) extract and compounds. *Planta medica, 58*(5), 417–423. https://doi.org/10.1055/s-2006-961504

Wu, C. C., Chuang, H. Y., Lin, C. Y., Chen, Y. J., Tsai, W. H., Fang, C. Y., Huang, S. Y., Chuang, F. Y., Lin, S. F., Chang, Y., & Chen, J. Y. (2013). Inhibition of Epstein-Barr virus reactivation in nasopharyngeal carcinoma cells by dietary sulforaphane. *Molecular carcinogenesis, 52*(12), 946–958. https://doi.org/10.1002/mc.21926

Yiang, L., Lian, W.M., Gang, Z. R., Mei, M. X., Qun, W., Yi, Z. (2013). The Induction of Epstein-Barr Virus Early Antigen Expression in Raji Cells by GSM mobile phone radiation. Biomed Envion Science. 26 (1): 76-78.

Yiu, C. Y., Chen, S. Y., Chang, L. K., Chiu, Y. F., & Lin, T. P. (2010). Inhibitory effects of resveratrol on the Epstein-Barr virus lytic cycle. *Molecules (Basel, Switzerland), 15*(10), 7115–7124. https://doi.org/10.3390/molecules15107115

Young, R. and Young, S. R. (2001) *Sick and tired: reclaim your terrain.* Pleasant Grove, UT: Woodland Publishing.

Zhao, L., Xie, F., Wang, T. T., Liu, M. Y., Li, J. L., Shang, L., Deng, Z.

X., Zhao, P. X., & Ma, X. M. (2015). Chlorpyrifos Induces the Expression of the Epstein-Barr Virus Lytic Cycle Activator BZLF-1 via Reactive Oxygen Species. *Oxidative medicine and cellular longevity, 2015*, 309125. https://doi.org/10.1155/2015/309125

Zhu, H., Wang, X., Shi, H., Su, S., Harshfield, G. A., Gutin, B., Snieder, H., & Dong, Y. (2013). A genome-wide methylation study of severe vitamin D deficiency in African American adolescents. *The Journal of pediatrics, 162*(5), 1004–9.e1. https://doi.org/10.1016/j.jpeds.2012.10.059

ABOUT THE AUTHOR

Candice Andrus, ND is a Board Certified Traditional Naturopath, Nutritional Therapist, and Ordained Spiritual Minister. Originally from Frankenmuth, MI, Candice has lived in Sarasota, FL since 1991. Since undergoing her own healing journey 20 years ago, she has been passionate about teaching people how to regain their health and get their life back. Candice is also a Certified Personal Trainer and Yoga Teacher, certified in Ayurveda Therapy, Yin Yoga and Standup Paddleboard Yoga. She has taught yoga to student athletes of all ages and professional athletes from all over the world at IMG Academy in Bradenton, FL since 2011 and has coached clients on nutrition, lifestyle and detoxification both independently and at Sarasota Integrative Health since 2013. She works with clients locally and remotely. Candice specializes in immune health, chronic illness, weight loss, mold illness, and emotional/spiritual roots of illness.

Printed in Great Britain
by Amazon

61519565R00038